The Myth in Marriage

Alice Hubbard

Table of Contents

FOREWORD

MRRIAGE is a subject of interest to all adults, and at one time in almost every life it is the vision that fills the horizon.

To many it is a mirage.

To a few it proves to be the hills from whence cometh their strength. The rising sun of romance tips every blade of grass, every leaf and flower and twig, with the mystery and miracle of color and perfume.

The noonday light reveals truth that the half-light of the dawn could not show.

And evening twilight garners all the richness of marriage.

The purpose of this book is to enlighten by bringing into the light of day experiences that must come into the lives of women and men.

—*Alice Hubbard.*

6

There is a time in every man's education when he arrives at the conviction that he must take himself for better, for worse, as his portion; that though the wide universe is full of good, no kernel of nourishing corn can come to him but through his toil bestowed on that plot of ground which is given to him to till.—*Emerson.*

ROMANCE

The object of love expands and grows before us to eternity, until it includes all that is lovely, and we become all that can love.—*Thoreau.*

MARRIAGE, although a most common incident in life, is understood as little as is birth, life and death. People are perpetually ignorant on the subject, and insist upon remaining in this state until the veil of their temple is rent in twain, and their holy of holies has daylight thrown upon it.

Love is a sacred mystery whose secret is as yet locked away from mortals. We recognize a few of its manifestations and dream of its power. We connect it in our thoughts with marriage and birth, but we assume its presence: we do not bring proof.

Love is spirit, and can not be analyzed nor understood.

The most that man can apprehend of it is to know its absence or its presence. Its most refined manifestations have come to us with the development of intellect.

There are only a few examples of the manifestation of great love in history. So rare are the people capable of its expression that the whole world wonders and in awe has said that the Creator is Love.

And lovers have been set apart as belonging to the Great Mystery and revered in degree as is the Source of Love.

One of the phases of this manifestation in people is the desire to give. The lover withholds nothing from his beloved. There is one desire—to give all. Thus is the mind expanded until it reaches truth never before seen.

Love is the enlightener of the soul. It is the all-seeing eye that discovers the highest possibilities in man. Its eternal desire is to fulfil these.

"I can do no ill, because I could not meet the beloved on terms of equality if there were any stain upon my soul. My hands and my heart must be clean."

Love's longing is to be entirely whole, clean and strong.

Love would never deceive. It is kindred only to truth and good.

All of life is sacred to the lover, and all life is sacred to him.

The lover is not so anxious that the beloved shall be perfect, as that she herself, he himself, shall be without blemish. Love purifies the lover. Love makes the lover clean.

There is no such thing as unrequited love, for to have loved is all the compensation there is. The soul asks no more.

There is a sublime dignity in love—a majesty that suggests unlimited power.

To love is an individual experience. The object of the love is only the means to this end of awakening and purification.

When the lover asks aught from the beloved, he has descended from the spiritual estate and begins to haggle and barter. Then it is not love, but becomes something to buy and sell with.

Love radiates from the individual, as rays of light from its source.

When the lover wants to continue the ecstacy of the experience of unselfishness, prolong the forgetfulness of his sordid self, he does what? Just the opposite of what will secure for him this Nirvana! He begins to demand. He asks her to be forever near him, she asks him to forever stay, all in faith, believing that the soul-awakener is a person, when the person has only reminded the soul of an ideal. For a time this person keeps this ideal living before the soul of the lover.

Elbert Hubbard says, "I love you because you love the things I love." There is a trinity in love. Lovers make the soul to see a similar ideal which both love.

So long as each asks nothing from the other, makes no demand, this ideal may continue to come before the mind, and remain there while the person is present, and return at the thought of the beloved.

THE REVELATION

The gay enchantment was undone,
A gentle wife, but fairy none.—Emerson.

THE ecstacy of feeling the presence of the ideal may continue for many meetings and partings, until the lovers believe that each is responsible for the beautiful ideal that is theirs.

They arrange to live permanently in each other's presence.

But this living together has induced a thousand conditions that had nothing whatever to do with the ecstacy of the soul.

Young people do not realize how much economics has to do with every-day living until they are face to face with every-day life.

Earning money, the drudgery in housework, the personal habits of the individuals, intimate tastes and prejudices, are all foreign to the awakening of ideals in the soul. The beloved, who was once an angel, becomes a wife, a weaver, a worker, a plain human being, subject to the shortcomings and ignorance that other human beings have.

And the lover, who is also beloved, becomes a husband, an earner of money, in competition with other workers, subject to irritation, weariness, discouragements, human failings.

The human qualities, the frailties and shortcomings, do not inspire the soul to high ideals. And each looks across the impassable gulf of the breakfast-table and wonders why they "introduced into their lives a spy."

"Where is the ideal I was to dwell with?"

"Where is the ideal that was to abide with me?"

Their souls are wrenched in anguish.

FACTS

You must stand up straight and put a name upon your actions.—Stevenson.

THE business in marriage requires commonsense about ninety-nine per cent.

There is usually less romance in marriage than in any other relationship of life.

But the general idea concerning marriage is that it is all or nearly all romance.

There is no other business partnership so intimate and complex as that in marriage.

And this partnership is entered into, the legal papers are drawn, witnesses to the transaction are called, and a life agreement is made without thought, discussion or an agreement concerning the business part of this partnership.

Emphasis has been placed only upon the love, the part of the contract which mortals can not control.

The business part of this contract holds the destinies of the contracting parties as no other partnership can. Husband and wife can ruin each other's fortunes utterly. No outsider can do this.

We would consider two men ridiculous who entered into a business partnership, discussing with each other only the pleasure they anticipated in seeing each other so constantly as they would, working side by side each day.

Imagine one partner saying to the other, "With all my worldly goods I thee endow," and slipping upon his finger a little gold ring. Then for the duration of this partnership, the privileged partner giving to him who wears the ring what he is inclined, varying as the joy in each other's presence waxes or wanes. The idea is silly.

And yet a man and a woman may contract to live together, giving little serious thought to the business part of such living, until they find that mortals can not live on romance, and that the joy of their lives has flown away.

Ecstacy continued, burns up life, and is not intended except for inspiration.

Love may continue with marriage, and it may not. Civilization has drifted us into conditions where it is difficult for romance to continue after the lovers enter into the business of life

10

together.

Marriage is of universal interest. The weal or woe of the race is involved in it.

It is a natural incident in the lives of lovers; but the marriage of lovers, although an incident in love, becomes an event in their lives because of the business partnership, which phase they did not contemplate.

The primal purpose in the marriage of lovers is that they may be perpetually purified, that they may live constantly their best. To do this they must have the Ideal forever before them.

When the business part of marriage shows another "side" of their natures, the Ideal may take wings. Then they naturally feel they are cheated. Their first impulse is to run away from this "trouble," to get back to the Ideal before it has been effaced.

AN AWAKENING

Love, indeed, is light from heaven;
A spark of that immortal fire by Allah given.—Byron.

THE expressions, "falling in love," and "making love," are terms suggesting something that is impossible.

No one falls in love. The experience of loving may come when a person has evolved where fine perceptions are possible. All living is an awakening process in which there are many degrees of consciousness. At a certain stage in his evolution, a human being is able to see and feel certain truth.

The imagination is a power which is developed with intellect and fine feeling. The imagination can create a world and people it. In this way, ideals are perpetually made. Humanity's effort to realize ideals is evolution.

When man can image a human being that fulfils the highest ideal he can create, the soul rejoices. Man forgets the imperfect in his ecstacy when contemplating the perfect. And when one human being sees another human being who reminds him, more or less, of his ideal, he is said to love.

He does not "fall" nor "make," he realizes, he awakens, and sometimes re-creates.

It may often occur that the person who awakens one to this ideal may recall this ideal once, twice, again and yet again. Or this person may constantly recall it, or cease altogether to recall it.

That man and woman are lovers who constantly keep before each other the Ideal.

They wish to abide together, because together they live their best lives, do their best work, are most kind to their fellow-man, do no wrong, can do no wrong. This is commonly accepted today as the basis of marriage. It is this ideal which is vaguely or definitely in the minds of thinking people when they wish to marry.

The poet Dante had a wonderful, complete ideal. He saw but twice the woman who reminded him of his Perfect. He wrote in poetry of his Ideal and called Her by this woman's name.

His wife, the mother of his children, was another woman.

Many critics say that Dante's love for Beatrice was pure. Probably they say this, because he asked nothing of her. That he never knew Beatrice was fortunate, for the two people had very little in common. Dante was a poet and dreamer. Beatrice was a woman

12

of the nobility without serious cares and responsibilities.

THE NATURAL MARRIAGE

Cell seeks affinity with cell.—Reedy.

WHEN young people meet on a natural basis our present civilization insists that it must necessarily be followed by a permanent, life-long friendship or disgrace.

The cosmic urge causes a meeting which, if followed by an enforced close relationship, usually has incompatability as a sequence.

Nature has one thing forever in mind. Civilization has not counted on this.

A youth and a maiden meet when passion is strong, the will undisciplined and judgment undeveloped. Convention says there is but one thing to do when young people are thus strongly attracted to each other, and that is to get the sanction of society (church and state) and make arrangements for a permanent intimacy.

The youth expects the perpetual beauty, smile and charm of the ballroom, reception or parlor. The maiden expects protestation of love, and her ideals and promises fulfilled.

Each has firmly fixed in the mind an idea of something that has none or little of the real in it—an idea that is impossible. Yet in it there are hope and fond desire somewhere hinted.

The facts are that a struggle has just begun with some of the unpoetic realities of existence, of which neither has ever before dreamed.

Perhaps the wife must rise early, prepare the breakfast, keep the rooms in order. This is work.

The husband goes to business.

Business perplexes.

"Oh, she is just like other women!"

"Oh, he is just a common man!"

They complain.

The cosmic urge has nothing to do with any of this. It has come—and gone, perhaps.

There is left a social situation. These two young people have had something in common, and possibly only a transitory something.

How shall they live together when she loves what he hates, and he has hopes, ambitions, desires that are nothing to her?

14

"He has cheated me!" "She has fooled me!" is their heart-cry.

The truth, however, is something like this: "We have been deceived. Nature said one thing to us, and we confused with it something else and thought what society said was true. We have been deceived."

There was nothing in the first attraction that made these two understand anything about hardships, disagreeable duties, discomforts, weariness, pain.

Those who are anxious to uphold church authority are saying a good deal about the divorce evil. They bring statistics to show that one out of every twelve marriages results in divorce.

They have not, however, secured any statistics as to whether the people in the other eleven marriages enjoy what our Constitution affirms to be the rights of American citizens: life, liberty and the pursuit of happiness.

The Church is talking about a "cure" for the divorce evil! One bishop earnestly recommends the Jewish anathematization, "Let neither party ever be spoken to again." But how would this remedy the social condition of the two?

This is punishment, but not cure. The cause of the trouble is not even looked for by the bishop.

"Is marriage a failure?" According to the divorce-courts it is.

The Church concedes that one-twelfth of all marriages are failures.

THE SOCIAL MARRIAGE

I am not surprised that some make shipwreck, but that any come to port.—Stevenson.

A SOCIAL marriage is based on the idea of a high and lofty friendship, an indissoluble partnership, an intimacy of relationship unknown in any other phase of existence.

Such a marriage was not intended by Nature. A new element is introduced when a social marriage occurs of which Nature had no thought, and we should reckon with this, not without it.

This new element is the intellect. Nature does not recognize it in the cosmic urge. So the meeting of man and woman on an intellectual plane, on a basis of the sweetest friendship imaginable, is the only condition by which Nature can endure the social marriage tie—which so often binds, imprisons, and makes slaves.

Even at this time man considers that he owns a woman; that he has purchased her freedom, her will, her habits, her aspirations, her time, her love, her energies, her future, every activity of her life. She is in very truth under a master. And the woman, as well, usually considers this true.

The woman thinks, because she is owned, that there are certain rights connected with her husband which she also has. In the majority of cases the wife realizes her inferior strength when might makes right, and the husband is not trusted. He must give an account of himself, morning, noon and night; of his money, his letters, his attentions.

The woman has certain laws which she, too, tries to enforce. He must support her, with all that the term implies.

"Didn't he promise to do this on the wedding-day?" Certainly, yes! So far as I know, humanity is one in its nature, and neither male nor female. No woman naturally wants to be owned and possessed. Humanity rebels against tyranny; and there is more discord, more heartaches, more wrangling, more unhappiness among married people than among the unmarried.

Were it possible for men and women when they marry to realize that they own nothing more in "rights" after marriage than they did before, and would make no more demands upon each other, marriage even with its present accepted meaning would not be a failure.

16

The import of marriage, as it is understood today, is on the basis of intellectual friendship, a business partnership, mutuality in all interests of life. Few people know this.

We have mixed methods. Nature makes no compulsory laws in this matter of living together.

Society has done this. The laws man makes, man must enforce. But what God hath joined together, no man can put asunder. What God hath not joined together, man is not very successful in combining.

We have demonetized woman, taking away from her the natural strength, courage and independence that belong to the mother; made of her a slave, under which condition she does not thrive.

And neither does man thrive in being master, for the chain that holds the one is fastened to the wrist of the other.

Woman must make herself economically free, find work that exercises her body and her mind, and most of the cause of discord, unrest and unhappiness will have disappeared.

THE MARRIAGE OF CONVENIENCE

Its only end is the principle of existence.—Disraeli.

PEOPLE who marry without ideals entering in as part of the contract have few disappointments or troubles.

If the woman expects the man simply to provide shelter, food, raiment, and the man expects a good cook, housekeeper and valet, and each fulfils his part of the expectation, there are few other demands.

Tenderness, kindness, attentions are asked for very moderately, and good service brings its own reward. Each understands the situation and has accepted this business arrangement with marriage. So there is no disappointment, no heartache. They get out of their marriage all they had expected. They are not guilty of experiment and folly. They have their quota of commonsense—and use it. Their ideals are simple and easily attained.

CONCLUSION

We two have climbed together,
Maybe we shall go on yet, side by side.—Schreiner.

LOVERS who marry think more of the Ideal than of all else. And if or when the Ideal ceases to remain in the presence of the husband or the wife, then love is gone. In its place sorrow sits.

Whatever marriage may have been in the past, it has now two distinct phases which should be definitely understood by all people.

I. The business partnership.
II. The spiritual relation.

THE BUSINESS OF MARRIAGE

You are dealing with something far more precious than any plant—the priceless soul of a child.—Burbank.

THE civic recognition of marriage does not take direct cognizance of the Ideal, or love-phase, of this unilateral contract, although it assumes that love is the motive of the union. The state takes it for granted that the purpose of this union is to perpetuate the race, give to the state citizens. The permanence of the marriage is supposed to be desirable, because the physical support and welfare of wife and children rests with the husband, unless he become insane, sick or criminal.

Then Charity gives the pauperizing support of a tyrant. Desirable citizens are seldom evolved in "Institutions."

Occasionally, a mother is endowed with power to maintain her family alone; but the instances are few.

In marriage the state obtains the promise of the contracting parties to love, honor and cherish; to love, honor and obey, through sickness, through health, until death.

However, the state is able to enforce but one portion of the promise, "to cherish," which, being interpreted, means that the husband must contribute a certain portion of his income to the woman, provided she has not broken the letter of the law in one respect, and has not deserted nor flagrantly quarreled with her husband. If she has been acquiescent, she is still to be "cherished." This alimony, as such tax is sometimes termed, is required whether the wife is mother or not, or is engaged in educating citizens or not. It may be exacted—the letter of the law—although the intent of the marriage may not have been fulfilled.

Tacitly, the state recognizes the desirability of love in marriage, although it has no jurisdiction over it, and can not enforce the keeping of this promise by husband or wife.

Loving or not loving is not within the control of mortals.

It is admitted now by men and women that the laws of all countries of the world were made by men for men. They do not discriminate against women so seriously and so unjustly as did Moses, but the civil laws give wife and mother no chance for independence.

Until recently, the promise to obey has been enforced; also,

20

the wife's promise to be true to one man and none other. So we have had the prayer which is international: "Make our women virtuous and our men brave," the meaning of brave being, able to fight man and beast.

"Virtue" has been interpreted as being a negation, an indifference to all but husband.

Nothing that can transpire in wedlock is considered not virtuous.

"Oh, Liberty! Liberty! What crimes are committed in thy name!"

Woman has found submission easier than to assert and obtain the human right of independence in the control of her own mind and body.

"It is a hard world for girls," said Martin Luther, five hundred years ago.

It is still a hard world for girls and women.

Nature is said to love the female more than the male, for she serves Her more devotedly, and Nature has taken care that she shall.

PRIMITIVE BONDAGE

Woman pays the first cost on human life.—Schreiner.

WHEN a woman feels the first grip of her child's dependence upon her, she has forever lost her freedom. If the child dies, a grave shackles her soul through life. If the child lives, the welfare of that child keeps perpetually between her and the sun.

Before her babe is born, Nature has absorbed the mother's strength and charm that Her one purpose may be accomplished. Man finds it easy to neglect woman then. In fact, his honor, pride, fear and loyalty to a principle, one or all, are his safeguard and the mentor that holds him to duty when his wife is absorbed by motherhood.

Nature demands all from the mother. She takes possession and uses her so that the woman has no will for the time. She is Nature's, body and soul, "Used by an unseen Power for an unknown end."

Does a woman enter into this prison-house voluntarily?

Never.

Nature blindfolds and lures her into it.

Before civilization developed a hectic super-sentiment in woman, she lived as do the animals. Naturally, motherhood was an incident in her life. Her children early became independent, and she had a comfortable, healthy indifference to their welfare after they were able to get a living.

All the time she was a mother she was economically free. She had had the strength to take care of herself from childhood, and when her child came, she was able to care for both.

The father of her baby made no demands upon her for service as cook, housekeeper, laundress, valet, lover or friend. He took care of himself wholly, and so did she. All they wanted was food and shelter.

But since man's needs are multiple, the demands upon male and female are great.

NATURE'S METHOD

The more intimately we attach ourselves to Nature, the more she glows with beauty and returns us our affection.—Froebel.

NATURE does not seem to have expected man to get more than a primitive living. She has not changed Her methods at all.

Man has changed. He makes and directs machinery that earns for one man what fifty men can earn; so that one man is fifty times richer than a primitive man.

Nature uses no machinery.

It takes more than twenty years of the mother's time to develop one citizen. There are no short cuts nor quick methods in woman's special work.

The mother of a large family has given twenty-five of the best years of her life to the work which none but her can do.

She has given to the state citizens.

This has cost her all her strength, all her time and the ambitions of a quarter of a century.

As our present civilization is, she has given her economic independence, her individual ambitions.

She pays dearly for the privilege of being mother to citizens. She is dependent upon one man for the maintenance of both herself and her children.

THE man, too, is blindfolded by Nature and is led where he knows not.

The desire to give all of his earnings to the development of citizens may never have been his. He may not know nor care about the welfare and perpetuation of the state.

But Nature has not bound him hand and foot to Her plans. When, or if, his affection ceases for this woman who is dependent upon him for food, shelter and clothing, he may use his own judgment about the woman's and the children's needs. So long as they escape the attention of the Humane Societies, the family is at his mercy. The woman and her work are dependent upon him just the same.

Unwilling money buys poor food, clothing and teaching. It has evolved bargain-days and cheap goods.

ECONOMIC FREEDOM

She considereth a field and buyeth it. With the fruit of her hands she planteth a vineyard.—Solomon.

THE wisdom of stateswomen and of statesmen should evolve a sure foundation-fund, whereby mothers shall have a solid financial basis for doing woman's work.

Civilization has placed a ban upon motherhood. There is ever the stigma upon it which Moses placed there. It is hard, cruelly hard, to be a mother in the United States, this "land of the free."

We anathematize and practically kill a mother who has not conformed to our laws, irrespective of what Nature has said about it. We take her child from her, hide it, falsify about it, and then disown the mother if she demands the inherent rights of a mother.

We talk about the glory of motherhood, but we do not act to the glory of motherhood.

The business of marriage is to develop citizens. The financial part of this partnership should receive the most careful attention of all people who are to marry. They should realize that they are assuming responsibilities great and unknown to them. They are leaving a simple life to enter into one vastly more complex.

Woman is fast evolving a brain. And women are thinking. Brain, not sentiment, will be the directing power under which women live. Wisdom and judgment will guide them. They will not give the best in their lives to the work of rearing children, without reasonable, business assurance of funds with which to do their work.

CITIZENS

It is true that I am an alien.

But my son—my son is Themistocles.—Euterpe.

A CITIZEN is one who has evolved from a condition where he was content to live alone, care for himself alone, into a state where he desires to live with others, and is interested in the welfare of others.

Women were the first human beings to qualify as citizens.

Their care for their children early extended their interest beyond their own welfare. From protecting and providing for her immediate family, the mother's interests naturally extended first to all children and then to all human beings who were in need of care.

Women are potential mothers, and so are inherent citizens.

Women are citizens by natural tendency.

Men are citizens by education.

The desire to co-operate is the natural desire of an evolving, sane people. Supremely selfish people, who care not at all for others, are either barbaric or insane.

A city was the result of the citizen instinct.

The mother's brain was evolved through her desire to benefit her children. She then saw that what was good for her own was good for her neighbor's family, and for all families. All manufactories, all industries, reforms and civic improvements have originated in woman's brain, evolved because of the mother-instinct of love.

From the city, human interest extended into the state, from the state into the nation. From the limitation of belonging to a nation, we shall sometime become citizens of the world.

A stateswoman or statesman is one who is intelligently active in work that materially benefits the citizens of a state or nation.

The rights of citizenship naturally belong to all people who wish to and can contribute to the welfare of their fellow-man.

Formerly statesmen were businessmen of experience and ability who had prescience. They could see what was beneficial to their own interests, and from this their interest expanded, and they saw what was good for the well-being of many men. They were men, like Benjamin Franklin, who were able to project themselves into the lives of others. They were the first monists.

26

Statesmen had had experience—they had lived. They knew values, what served and what was not desirable. They also knew that no one reaches any goal alone. No man can progress much faster than the rest of his kind.

So the statesman was a representative man, but a pioneer in progress. His avocation was to work for his kind. His vocation was his own business, which he minded very carefully.

Appreciative people saw the benefit to others, and gave the statesman the recognition of honors. This was all he desired or needed. He was not a pauper, he was not submerged in financial difficulties. The oppressed can not see beyond their own needs—are incapable of generous thoughts or wise judgment.

Statesmen were and are strong, successful men. People want for a savior one who can first save himself.

There came a time when statesmen, like lawyers, received pay for services rendered.

And lo, politicians and grafters, plums and taxes!

Today, statesmen are few and are classed as politicians.

All political offices have a little twig of laurel tied to the door, but the pay-envelope inside is generally what lures men to enter and abide. "The laborer is worthy of his hire," they affirm. And he is, provided he labors for the thing for which he was hired.

"The people" are willing to pay politicians for piecework, provided the quality is right.

When we say, "Children are the greatest asset of the nation," everybody nods assent to the sentiment, and many applaud.

"What we do with the children decides what they will do with the nation," we add, and there is never a dissenting look or voice.

We affirm that the greatest work the state can do is to develop citizens. Perpetuity of the state is synonymous with perpetuity of the race. This is supposed to be Nature's dearest desire—to perpetuate the race.

So it should be the dearest desire of statesmen, politicians, to perpetuate the state, and the state is the aggregation of its citizens.

We are in a dense fog with regard to the value of citizens.

We say that man is all. This is lip-service.

Politicians are interested in acquiring and holding power, in war appliances and armies. They give some assistance in the development and care of vegetables, fruits, trees, and the flora in general. They are also interested in the development of all domesticated animals, the preservation of the birds, forests and natural parks, the protection of the fish. They have game-laws which are wise and whose results are beneficial.

And the state hires and pays people to take care of all these interests. It also hires and pays people who see that the laws are respected which have been made for the protection and perpetuity of flora and fauna.

But as yet, lawmakers, politicians, reformers, and influential citizens have not made provision for the development of citizens, except as the institution of the school system assists in this work.

ENFORCED DEPENDENCE

Thou givest man bread. Let my aim be to give man himself.—Froebel.

THERE was a time when women, like statesmen, were economically free. They spun and wove, manufactured, planted, harvested, cooked. Land was cheap and needs were few. The women gave a part of their time to the state in rearing citizens, but they did not give all. They were self-supporting, in great measure; therefore, self-respecting and capable.

But women lost their economic independence when industries were taken from the home.

Farming, dairying, spinning, weaving, tailoring, laundering, baking, dressmaking, millinery, building, carpentering, are all done on a big scale, outside of the home, where the women, because they were mothers, could not follow their industries.

Women are left with the dependent occupations of working for the state and working for their husbands, for neither of which can they collect money.

Husbands' policy is: Where the treasury is, there will the wives' hearts be also.

The welfare of the women who give their time—twenty-four hours of the day, and for twenty-five or thirty years of their lives, their prime—for the development of citizens has been left to chance.

The state has made no provision whereby potential citizens shall be assured of the proper care.

The mother's time has been considered of no value, that is, her service is not paid for in money.

If, in her youth, a woman married a man who was able to make money, she might be assured of food, clothing and shelter for her children unless or until Fortune frowned and the property was lost.

Any woman, whose husband dies, gives her time to the care of her children, no matter how poorly equipped she may be to earn a living for them in the world. She tries to do her own work, and besides that, what her husband did—maintain the family.

The state has made no provision for the care of potential citizens whose father has died, thereby cutting off the income which was once theirs.

We say that the purpose of the home is to develop children, that the home is established for children.

The purpose of the school is to supplement the teaching of the home, and this is to be re-enforced by the influence of the church. The office of the state is to wisely protect the home and safeguard the interests of its citizens. The government is the mentor of the citizens.

The theory is admitted that the business world is organized and operated for the one purpose of maintaining the home and its adjuncts—school, church and government. But the fact is, that, except for the taxes which great business institutions pay, there are very few children taken care of directly by big businesses.

The very rich have one, possibly two, rarely three children, and these, instead of being developed for working citizens, often evolve into ornaments, and sometimes become a nuisance and an expense to the state.

The mothers who give their time to the care of large families have no regular incomes. Their husbands are poor, and contribute to the development of citizens what they can, or will.

The people who are doing the most important work for the state, for whom all business is operated (as tradition sayeth), have no capital, and are carrying on their more or less great work by donations, given at the discretion of the donor. They can not receive more than their husband's income, and never have that amount.

No matter how efficient these women may be as mothers, there is no recognition of this excellence, except by a few friends of the family.

Nothing has been done to make a large family popular. The trend of the whole course of civilization has been and is to do anything but evolve citizens.

Of course, women are supposed to be too spiritually minded to want compensation in money for work done for love.

However, is any great work done that is not done for love of the work? No one writes, paints, plays, builds, prints, binds books, models in leather or clay, raises cattle, fruits, grains, but him who loves his work. There is little response in any part of life, other than to love.

All workers accept the world's custom of using money as a medium of exchange for their time and energy—all except mothers and wives. So much service is given for so much money, and so much money for so much service.

Women are human beings, no more and no less than are men. They are just as human as men. They love freedom, independence and justice.

There is no natural reason why they should not have public recognition for work and development.

The custom of the world is to use money as a medium of exchange or as a representation of wealth. Wealth is an accumulation of energy held in reserve. People should be very careful to use this reserve advantageously. They are very jealous of expending time and energy unless it counts in wealth.

All people but mothers do this. This is why motherhood has become unpopular and a burden. The mother is in economics a pauper, a dependent, at the mercy or bounty of one man.

The first use of a home was to care for children, to protect them. Women built the first houses and for this one purpose.

Modern houses are made for adults more than for children. They are places of luxury. The thought of a nursery is seldom in the minds of the makers of houses. The architect does not have for his recurring theme, "How will this add to the development of citizens?"

Women are human beings. They are very much like men. They need recognition.

Self-preservation is the first law. And women, like men, are selfish. They often stifle the instincts of Nature in one direction that they may live in the world as it is today.

Rapid travel, the opportunity to see and know what there is to be seen and known, lures women just the same as it does men. Independence is just as dear to women as it is to men.

HOMOGENEITY

What we request of life is that the tools should be given to his hand or hers who can handle them.—Schreiner.

WOMAN is a human being before she is a mother and all the time she is a mother. And after her active work of motherhood is finished, she will still be a human being, subject to all the ambitions, hopes, desires and interests that humanity has.

Daughters have inherited tendencies from their fathers as well as from their mothers, and all daughters have done this from prehistoric times to the present. Sons have belonged to mothers as well as to fathers. The race is one.

Women can not be limited in the expression of this great miracle of life which stirs her soul, as it stirs man's.

Woman and man are awakening, brain and heart.

Woman must have freedom to work, to think, to find happiness, to express herself. She must be accepted as a part of every part of this becoming Democracy. She must be accepted in the world as it is today. She belongs, not to the past, but to this present.

There is work that she alone can do, and to do this she must be economically free.

The freedom of woman is the most important of all subjects that statesmen and citizens can consider.

Pay mothers for the work they do for the state. Give them the opportunity for economic freedom, that they may be self-respecting, and develop on equal terms with men.

The great need of the world is for better women and men—an evolving race.

There is just one way: we must have evolving mothers.

Servile mothers have slave sons and stupid daughters, and sometimes criminal children.

Women must be free to choose their occupations.

If they marry, they must recognize the business in marriage and enter into the business partnership with true intelligence.

With no less intelligence must men understand that the contract in marriage can not be unilateral and bring benefit or happiness to either person, nor can the purpose of marriage be best accomplished.

32

Democracy in marriage is the Great Imperative. We would have a democratic form of government? Democracy must begin at the foundation of all government—the home.

ROMANCE

We are ministered unto by the moonbeams and the starlight as well as by the god of day.

ROMANCE is the color and the perfume of life. It is that which gives charm to living. Romance lures us to live. It called us into being, has bound us to life, and does not desert us at its close.

Although Romance is the most intangible thing in the world, the moonshine of living, it is the most real.

It is the will-o'-the-wisp that has led to all invasions, all discoveries, all victories, all heroism, all inventions, all arts, all business, all human endeavor. Without it there would be no marriage. The human race would cease to be.

One of the myths in marriage is to assume that the Romance is all, or will continue under all conditions.

Business belongs to the realm of fact and deals with tangible substances. It has to do with the practical part of life. It gives us food, clothing, shelter. It furnishes us great problems, exercise for body and mind. It is a great factor in the evolution of man.

One of the myths in marriage is to assume that business and business struggles do not enter into the lives of lovers. The fact is that business occupies much of the time of every honest man and honest woman. It is necessary to life. Without work, romance would cease, the human race would die.

The ideal and the real are interdependent in all phases of human life.

In marriage there is a myth that the twain are one flesh. But the two are two, just as surely as one and one make two, unless neither is worth counting.

It might not be such folly for a woman to trust her happiness to a man, if any man could make any woman happy. But happiness is within the power of the individual alone. Nature intended it to be so.

If a woman were an incompetent, unable to earn or provide for herself, it might be well to leave her finances wholly in the hands of her husband.

But women who have the right to give children to society are capable of taking care of themselves and financing their personal interests.

34

Mothers should be thus capable.

In marriage we must recognize the individuality in the partnership, just as we must the romance and the facts.

A helpless, dependent, undeveloped, sentimental woman is not an inspirer of ideals. The man absorbed and involved in business is not an awakener or reminder of the Perfect.

A little time is necessary for the appreciation of the beautiful, the charming, the wonderful in life.

Leisure to think together and work together on things of mutual interest, is necessary to marriage, or there can be little love.

When lovers are independently dependent upon each other, it is a wonderful privilege to meet.

When lovers are economically free, as they were before marriage, there is no asking of favors nor demanding rights.

When lovers are grateful for the privilege of being together, and meet only when it is a joy to do so, love will abide.

And Romance, that lured them to life, and lighted their path to marriage, will ever illumine the way, even unto death.

If a woman's desire is to seek ease and luxury, and find oblivion, let her not marry, for that is not the easiest way thither. A woman has neither natural nor moral right to involve others in her selfishness.

If a man wants adoration, comfort, indulgence, cheap service and ease, let him not marry. He probably can get them all with more certainty and with less expense without marrying. A man has neither natural nor moral right to marry for these.

Men and women have not evolved far. "It doth not yet appear what we shall be."

Higher ideals will lure humanity on and on to a higher state of intelligence, and to better living, to a more refined and nobler justice than we have yet imagined.

Men and women will not long be looking for ease, nor want to have what they do not earn.

When love calls, they will respond with intelligence, knowing that this is Nature's voice, and therefore divine. They will rejoice in the most strenuous exercise of living.

Then with deep joy we can say at the close:

"To live is glorious. I have lived!"

www.ingramcontent.com/pod-product-compliance
Lightning Source LLC
Chambersburg PA
CBHW070103260726
48658CB00002B/962